Spot the difference
PIRATES!

© 2022 Webber Books

All rights reserved. This book or any portion thereof may not be reproduced or used in any manner whatsoever without the express written permission of the publisher except for the use of brief quotations in a book review.

CAN YOU SPOT THE 6 DIFFERENCES...?

A SHIP DOESN'T HAVE TO SAIL THE WAVES!

CAN YOU SPOT THE 7 DIFFERENCES...?

IT'S A PIRATE PARTY ME HEARTIES!

CAN YOU SPOT THE **7** DIFFERENCES...?

CAN YOU SPOT THE 8 DIFFERENCES...?

THE BIRDS LOVE TO SAIL ON A PIRATE SHIP!

CAN YOU SPOT THE 8 DIFFERENCES...?

CAPTAINS FIGHT FOR THE TREASURE CHEST!

CAN YOU SPOT THE 8 DIFFERENCES...?

TWO ISLANDS... BUT WHICH TO EXPLORE?

CAN YOU SPOT THE 8 DIFFERENCES...?

CAN YOU SPOT THE 8 DIFFERENCES...?

ARRR! LET'S MEET THE UNDERWATER PIRATES!

CAN YOU SPOT THE 9 DIFFERENCES...?

CAPTAIN'S COVE IS A POPULAR PLACE TO BE!

CAN YOU SPOT THE 9 DIFFERENCES...?

MOLLY MERMAID IS ABOUT TO LOSE HER GOLD!

SUNSET SHIPMATES... NEARLY TIME FOR BED!

CAN YOU SPOT THE 9 DIFFERENCES...?

THE FINAL PUZZLE... THANKS FOR PLAYING!

CAN YOU SPOT THE 10 DIFFERENCES...?

ANSWERS!

Check to see how many differences you found!

THE END!

www.ingramcontent.com/pod-product-compliance
Lightning Source LLC
Chambersburg PA
CBHW050758110526
44588CB00002B/43